Action Sports

In-Line Skating

John Martin

Capstone Press

MINNEAPOLIS

Printed in the United States of America.

Capstone Press • 2440 Fernbrook Lane • Minneapolis, MN 55447

Editorial Director   John Coughlan
Managing Editor   John Martin
Copy Editor   Theresa Early
Editorial Assistant   Michelle Wood

Library of Congress Cataloging-in-Publication Data

Martin, John, 1968-
    In-line skating / John Martin.
        p. cm.-- (Action Sports)
    Includes bibliographical references and index.
    ISBN 1-56065-202-0 (lib. bdg.)
    1. In-line skating--Juvenile literature. I. Title. II. Series.
GV859.73.M37 1994
796.2' 1--dc20   93-40644
                                                    CIP
                                                    AC

ISBN: 1-56065-202-0

99 98 97 96 95 94   8 7 6 5 4 3 2 1

Table of Contents

Chapter 1
A Look at In-Line Skating

The world zips by in a blur. You feel motion, speed, and excitement. You are enjoying the fastest-growing sport of the 1990s, in-line skating.

Millions of people around the world have taken to the pavement for the fun and excitement of in-line skating.

In-line skating has come a long way since 1760.

Chapter 2

The History of In-Line Skating

No one knows for sure who invented the first in-line skate. Many people credit an Englishman, Joseph Merlin. In 1760 he crafted wooden wheels and fitted them to his leather shoes.

These early skates were not perfect. They had no **brakes**. One day, trying to impress his friends, Merlin skated into a party while playing a violin. His entrance did not go as planned. He crashed into and shattered an expensive crystal mirror.

People of all ages enjoy the healthful sport of in-line skating.

In-Line Skating Today

The inventors of the modern in-line skate were two brothers from Minneapolis, Minnesota. In 1980 Scott and Brennan Olson wanted to practice ice hockey in the summer. They made wheels of polyurethane (a material like plastic) to replace the blades on their hockey skates.

10

The Olsons found that the new wheels acted on pavement much like a blade does on ice. Soon other people wanted to own in-line skates, too. The brothers started a company called Rollerblade, Inc. Since then in-line skating has skyrocketed in popularity. Rollerblade, Inc., is now the largest seller of in-line skates.

The Olsons also invented a type of in-line skate called Switch-It. It can double as an ice skate when its wheels are replaced by a skate blade.

Forms of In-Line Skating

In 1760, no one could have guessed in-line skating would become so popular. Today, people of all ages use their in-line skates in speed skating, artistic skating, freestyle skating, ramp skating, and roller hockey.

Safety equipment includes wrist guards, elbow pads, knee pads, and helmets.

Chapter 3

Basic Equipment

The in-line skates used today are faster, safer, and more comfortable than earlier models.

An in-line skate has five basic features: a shoe-like **shell**, a **liner**, a **frame**, **wheels**, and a brake.

The Shell

The shell supports the skater's ankles and keeps the skater's legs directly above the line of the wheels. It usually is made of either polyurethane or leather. Some shells are made of both.

Laces, buckles, or Velcro straps are used to tighten the shell around the foot. The shell should not be too stiff. It must be made to fit securely around the skater's entire foot and ankle.

The Liner

The soft, padded liner provides comfort and protects the skater's foot from impact.

The Frame

The frame holds the wheels in line and is attached to the shell. Generally, the frame is made of plastic reinforced with fiberglass. Some skaters use aluminum or metal-**alloy** frames for racing.

The Wheels

Wheels let the skater get into motion. The skater can choose the wheels' size and hardness.

When choosing wheels, skaters must consider their own ability, their weight, and the type of skating they practice.

Softer wheels are recommended for beginning skaters and skaters who weigh less than 100 pounds (45 kilograms). They "stick" to pavement better than hard wheels.

The skate consists of the shell, the liner, the frame, the wheels, and the brake.

For everyday skating, softer wheels provide the smoothest, safest ride. They will easily pass over pebbles or cracks in the pavement.

Roller hockey players and racers need harder wheels.

The Brake

The brake is a hard rubber block on the rear of one or both skates. If only one skate of your pair has a brake, that is the **brake skate.**

To stop, the skater leans back slightly to put the rubber brake against the pavement. The brake slows the skater by rubbing against the ground. The harder the skater presses the brake to the ground, the faster the stop.

Buying In-Line Skates

Be sure to buy quality skates. Good skates have a comfortable nylon liner, a stiff shell and frame, and polyurethane wheels that spin freely.

Expect to spend $100 to $400 for a good pair.

Poor-quality skates make it harder to learn to skate. They may even be dangerous. Bad skates have thin plastic shells that offer little ankle support, liners that wear out quickly, and wheels that spin less easily after several skating sessions.

Safety Gear

You also need protective gear. A full set

includes wrist guards, elbow pads, knee pads, and a helmet.

You can never tell when you might fall. A patch of water or a pebble can put even the most experienced skater down on the pavement.

Wearing the right protective gear lessens the chance of scrapes, bruises, bumps, or broken bones.

Speed skaters use skates with harder wheels and stiff aluminum or metal-alloy frames.

Chapter 4

Getting Started

After a few practice sessions, you will be surprised how easy in-line skating has become. Take it easy at first and be patient. Trying too much too soon can lead to accidents.

Finding the Right Place

In the city, it's easy to find a place to in-line skate. Any paved surface without dangerous traffic will work.

Parking lots, side streets, bike paths, sidewalks, and playgrounds are good places to in-line skate. For a really smooth ride, try an indoor roller rink.

Pick an area that is large, smooth, flat, and does not have many people around. Learning to balance is hard enough. You don't need a hill or traffic or lots of other people to make it harder.

Skating Obstacles

There is no such thing as perfect pavement. Watch out for cracks, pebbles, and wet or oily spots.

Cracks and pebbles do not let your skates glide freely. They can cause you to lose your balance.

On the other hand, oil and water can make the pavement slippery. They can make your skates slide out from under you.

You'll be surprised how easy and fun in-line skating becomes after just a few skating sessions.

Chapter 5

Basic In-Line Skating

It is time to start **blading**. Begin by bending your knees. Center your weight directly over your skates. Do not lean too far forward or backward. Your skates might slip out from under you.

Pushing Off

In this stance, you are ready to **push off**. For balance, bend your arms and keep your hands out in front of you at waist level. Place your arms in the same position as when you ride a bike.

Now push to the outside and back with one leg, keeping the other skate facing forward. The push propels you forward and sets you into

These skaters demonstrate the rhythmic movement of "pushing off."

motion. Next, make the same movement with the other leg.

As you become comfortable doing this, you will develop a rhythm of pushing and gliding.

To put force into each stride, push from all the wheels on the skate. This also helps you keep your balance.

Stopping

The best ways to slow your roll are the **heel stop** and the **T-stop**.

The Heel Stop

Bring the skate with the brake forward until the brake lines up with the toe of your other skate. Lift the toe of the brake skate until the brake touches the ground. Push hard until you roll to a stop.

The T-Stop

A more advanced way to stop is called a T-stop. While gliding along, the skater turns one skate outward and drags its wheels on the pavement. The two skates make a "T" shape together.

All the wheels of the back skate drag and bring you to a halt. This stop might seem as if it would ruin the wheels of your skates. Don't worry. They can take it.

Turns

Because of their narrow wheels, it is easier to make turns on in-line skates than on conventional roller skates. Just put in-line skates on edge and you go into a turn without even thinking about it.

There are two basic types of turns, the **glide turn** and the **crossover turn**. Beginners can learn glide turns quickly. Crossover turns take more skill.

Glide Turns

For a glide turn, a skater turns much the same way a skier would on snow. While the skier uses the skis' edges, the skater uses the wheels' edges.

For a right turn, keep your head facing right. Press on the inside edges of the wheels of the left skate. The harder you push with that skate, the sharper will be your turn to the right. Your right skate merely follows the left skate.

To make a glide turn to the left, put the pressure on the inside edges of the right skate.

Once you've mastered the basics, you can develop your own exciting style of in-line skating.

Crossover Turns

The crossover turn is for experienced bladers. It lets the skater turn more quickly than the glide turn. In-line racers use the crossover turn.

To do a left crossover turn, start into a glide turn. In the middle of the turn, put the right skate over and ahead of the left skate. To complete the turn, push off with the left foot.

For a right crossover turn, bring the left skate over and ahead of the right skate. Then push off

Speed skaters use the crossover turn to make quick, tight turns at speed.

with the right foot. Soon you'll be turning circles like a professional.

Skating Backward

Before long, everyone wants to skate backward. Skating backward is difficult to learn. It takes patience.

To begin, stand with your skates shoulder-width apart and your knees slightly bent. Point your toes inward and bring your knees together.

Now, keeping your weight on the inside edges of the skates, push outward with both skates. Keep pushing until your skates are just past your shoulders. You should begin to move backward very slowly.

Next, bring your skates back to their starting position by turning your heels inward and bringing your feet back together. Your wheels should stay on the ground at all times. Your weight should remain on the inside edges of the skates. Once you master this basic movement, skating backward is easy.

Chapter 6

Jumps and Extreme Skating

Extreme skating stretches the limits of skating. Extreme bladers develop original styles and try new things.

Extreme skating is for the experienced skater who has mastered the basics and is looking for a challenge.

The Basic Jump

Jumping is the first trick that extreme skaters learn. Only after you have mastered the **basic jump** should you go on to more advanced tricks.

Before jumping obstacles like this concrete pillar, start with objects that are a little more forgiving.

First find something to jump over. Something small, such as a soda pop can, works well to begin with.

Start about 50 feet (15 meters) away from the object. When you feel ready, skate straight toward it. Build up some speed. About 20 feet (6 meters) from the object, start to glide with your feet together. Tuck your body into a crouched position.

When to Jump

When to prepare for the jump depends on how fast you are going. The faster you go, the more space you need.

At medium speeds, five feet (1.5 meters) gives you enough room to make the jump. When you get that close, crouch a bit more. Push off with both skates right in front of the object. Jump as high as possible.

Try to land with your skates shoulder-width apart. If you need to, take a stride to regain your balance.

Gradually build up to more challenging jumps. Never jump anything that could hurt you if you do not clear it. A cardboard box collapses if you do not quite clear it. Fences, park benches, and bike racks are not good objects to jump.

Curb Jumping

In **curb jumping**, skaters move from the sidewalk into the street. However, you do not really jump. You just ride over the curb.

Before you curb jump, always check for cars. When you are sure the road is clear, glide toward the curb. Let your speed carry you off the curb and down to the street. Watch your balance.

Riding the Ramps

The most advanced extreme skating happens on ramps. Ramps let skaters fly high into the air and perform amazing spins and twists.

Do not take to a ramp until you can skate forward and backward, make crossover turns, and stop easily. Ramp riders also need the best safety equipment and quick reflexes.

Stair riding uses the same technique as curb jumping, but takes even keener balance.

Half-pipe skaters can "get a lot of air."

The best way to learn ramp skating is from an instructor certified by the Rollerblade In-Line Skating Association.

Types of Ramps

The most common type of ramp for in-line skating is the half-pipe ramp.

Many of the moves now practiced by in-line skaters were first performed by skateboarders who used half-pipe ramps for their tricks.

Half Pipes

Half pipes are, literally, half of a round pipe. The blader skates from one top edge or lip of the pipe to the other edge. The half pipe usually measures about 25 feet (7.6 meters) across.

Exhibitions usually use half-pipe ramps because they let the skater stay in constant motion and "get a lot of air." Skaters drop from one peak and pump their legs. This gives them the speed to reach the top edges or even beyond.

Two roller hockey forwards battle for the puck.

Chapter 7

Roller Hockey and Speed Skating

Many forms of in-line skating have developed, such as racing, extreme skating, and artistic skating.

Most recently, the sports of roller hockey and speed skating have become popular.

Popular Around the World

Roller hockey leagues have sprung up all over the world. National roller hockey teams compete against skaters from other countries in the World Championships and in the Pan American Games.

American Heather Laufer (25) leads the pack in the 1992 World Championships in Rome, Italy.

In 1992, roller hockey teams competed for the first time in the Summer Olympics.

Roller Hockey Basics

Roller hockey looks much like ice hockey. The rink is the same rectangular shape. There is a goal at each end. Players wear helmets, gloves, and **breezers** (padded shorts) just like ice hockey players.

Roller hockey players use ice hockey sticks. Sometimes a plastic roller hockey stick is used. The puck is made of a light plastic.

No body contact is allowed in roller hockey. The players rely on speed and skill to move the puck past the other team's players.

A typical roller hockey team is made up of five players: two forwards, a goaltender (the "goalie"), and two defensive players.

Speed Skating

Speed skating is a simpler sport. Speed skaters use a fast, five-wheeled skate and race as individuals, not as teams.

The race can be a sprint or as long as 30 kilometers (18.6 miles). Racers skate on oval tracks or cross-country along a twisting path.

In-line racing uses the basic skating technique. For extra speed and power, swing your arms side to side and bend forward a bit more. Always keep your legs pumping.

Chapter 8

Safety and Rules of the Road

The International In-Line Skating Association works to increase safety awareness among skaters. It has established in-line skating rules of the road. These rules are:

1. Wear safety equipment: wrist guards, knee and elbow pads, and helmet.

2. Stay alert and be courteous at all times.

3. Control your speed.

4. Skate on the right side of paths, trails, and sidewalks.

5. Overtake other pedestrians, cyclists, and skaters on the left. Tell others you are passing them by shouting, "Passing on your left."

6. Be aware of trail conditions: traffic, weather conditions, water, potholes, or storm debris.

7. Obey all traffic regulations. When on skates you must obey the same laws as cars, trucks, or cycles.

8. Stay out of areas with heavy automobile traffic.

9. Always yield to pedestrians.

10. Before skating any trail, learn the basic skills: turning, controlling speed, braking down hills, and avoiding obstacles.

Glossary

alloy–a mixture of different metals

blading–skating on in-line skates

brake–a rubber pad on the rear of a skate used to stop the skater

brake skate–the skate of a pair that has the brake pad on the back

breezers–uniform shorts worn by hockey players over protective pads

crossover turn–turning by bringing one foot across in front of the other

elbow pad–a cushion inside a hard shell that protects the elbow in a fall

extreme skating–skating that uses jumps, tricks, and fancy, showy moves

frame–the part of the in-line skate that holds the wheels

freestyle skating–skating that is not racing or performing set movements

glide turn–turning by tilting the skates and leaning into the turn

half pipe–a ramp shaped like a half circle or half a circular pipe

heel stop–stopping by tilting the skate to drag the brake pad along the ground

knee pad–a cushion inside a hard shell that protects the knee in a fall

liner–the padded layer that fits inside the shell of an in-line skate

ramp skating–using ramps to jump and gain speed for freestyle moves

roller hockey–a game similar to ice hockey, played on in-line skates

shell–the boot or outer skin of the in-line skate

speed skating–racing on a set course for a set distance on in-line skates

T-stop–stopping by dragging one skate sideways behind the other, to form a "T"

wrist guard–a pad with built-in supports to protect the wrist in a fall

To Learn More

Read:

Gutman, Bill. *Blazing Bladers*. New York, NY: Tor Books, 1992.

Joyner, Steven Christopher. *The Complete Guide and Resource to In-Line Skating*. Cincinnati, OH: Betterway Books, 1993.

Rappelfeld, Joel. *The Complete Blader*. New York, NY: St. Martin's Press, 1992.

Sullivan, George. *In-Line Skating, A Complete Guide for Beginners*. New York, NY: Cobblehill Books, 1993.

Watch:

Rollerblade Start 'N' Stop. Rollerblade, Inc., made this videotape to teach different in-line skating techniques. To get it, call Rollerblade, Inc.'s Consumer Service Hotline: (800) 232-ROLL.

Write to:

International In-Line Skating Association
Lake Calhoun Executive Center
3033 Excelsior Blvd., Suite 300
Minneapolis, MN 55416

Index

Photo Credits:

Rollerblade, Inc.: cover, pp. 6, 10, 12, 18, 24, 27, 30, 32, 35; Nathan Bilow © Allsport USA: p. 4; Jay Carroll: pp. 8-9; Ultra Wheels: pp. 15, 22, 38; U.S. Amateur Confederation of Roller Skating: pp. 17, 28, 40; Peter Ford Photography, p. 36.